PABLO PLATERO

WORKING ON HAPPINESS

Wellbeing and Personal Development

WORKING ON HAPPINESS

All Rights Reserved

Published by Pablo Platero

available at

V. 21382

Translation Martina Platero

First Edition

Copyright @2019, 2023

ISBN 979-862-32455-8-8

To Gaby

Table of Contents

Acknowledgments 9

Introduction 11

Happiness 19

PART 1: Manage your 40% 25

Gratitude 27
Purpose 32
Goal Setting 37
Positivity vs. Negativity 41

PART 2: Storms 45

Watch and stay calm 49
Stress management 52
Self-fulfilling prophecies 57

PART 3: Personal Change 63

The right question: How would you like to be? 67
Your best version 71
Time management 74
Meeting your goals 77
Help Others 81
Lead the change 86
Personal Impact 90

PART 4: Your Potential 95

Learn from your mistakes 99
Strengths 102
What you can't give up 107

Epilogue: You Choose 111

Acknowledgments

The process of writing this, my first book, has been as difficult as imperfect, and filled me with wonderful learnings. I am not an expert in psychology or neurosciences, but I am widely curious about the science of happiness and as such, I am a detailed observer of human behaviors.

I appreciate the enormous support in this adventure to my whole family, my wife Gaby, my children Martina, Gonzalo, and Felipe who teach me day in and day out what happiness is all about. Also, to my parents, to my brothers who have always been with me, and of course to my lifelong friends, those who from elementary school until today make me laugh to tears, filling my heart and my soul. Thanks for your unconditional friendship.

I thank all the people who educated me in this field, especially Tal Ben-Shahar from whom I have learned most of the concepts expressed in these pages through his lectures and books. Also, Maria Sirois and Megan McDonough along with so many other people who enlightened me with their magic.

Finally, I thank all the people I have worked with for almost thirty years, who helped me through good and bad examples to gain inspiration for this book.

Introduction

Am I happy? I've asked myself that question hundreds of times, and for many years I didn't get an straight answer. In fact, now I know I didn't even understand the meaning of the question. What's is happiness after all?

Being happy with the life we have is everyone's primary goal, isn't it? Then, how is it that something that is so relevant to every human being is so difficult to define? I will try to answer this question in the next few pages, but before that I want to briefly tell my personal story.

One day, soon after moving my family to Brazil, something happened that would change my life forever. That afternoon, my wife, Gaby, was exploring some additional training to complement her degree in Psychology to get better job opportunities at our new destination. She asked me to sit by her side and showed me the two main options she was evaluating, somehow expecting that my opinion could help her to decide. After reviewing the options for a few moments, I said: *"I find them both quite interesting for you to explore, but I think the one called Positive Psychology is fascinating. Actually, if you go ahead with that option, I'd love to join you. We could do this together."*

I will never forget her skeptical gaze, not understanding why I might be interested in something like that, but soon we were both excited to learn and share this experience together. It was the first time I had heard about Positive Psychology, known as "The Science of Happiness", and I loved it from the very first moment I read about it. Just a few hours later we had already paid the initial tuition fees and were ready to embark on that adventure.

What really triggered my impulse to study Positive Psychology was, perhaps, the need to answer some questions and most importantly to answer "the" question. I was dealing with that sort of permanent contradictory feeling since I had all what a man can desire, health, a fantastic family, good friends and a great job, but yet, I didn't feel I was flourishing and enjoying enough my life fully, probably driven by my worries about the uncertainties of the future or the rumination of past events.

The learning process to get our official Certificate lasted for a year, with a mix of virtual and immersive learning. It was a revealing and extraordinary experience. It allowed me to find some answers I've been looking for a long time, develop tools for improving my life and general well-being, and grow as an individual.

What is Positive Psychology? In a nutshell it is the scientific study of human flourishing, and an applied approach to optimal functioning. It has also been defined as the study of the strengths and virtues that enable individuals, communities, and organizations to thrive. In simpler words, it studies people, families and organizations that function well, that flourish and reach their full potential, unlike traditional psychology that focuses on problems, pathologies and dysfunctions.

We had the privilege of studying with Tal Ben-Shahar, who is famous for having designed and led the Positive Psychology course for Harvard, transforming it into the most popular class in the history of that prestigious University.

We also read lots of books on the subject and we enjoyed sharing learnings, thoughts and reflecting together. As parents we also practice with our children many of the concepts we learned.

But the most relevant thing for the purpose of this book is that I manage to put it into practice in my work environment, which helped me to create a healthier vision of myself as a professional, while also helping my colleagues to do so. Throughout my career I have observed that work has a significant importance in our lives and often is a determining factor for our lifestyle, our humor, our relationships and, in the long run, our happiness. This happens not only because we spend a significant number of hours in our jobs, but also because it is at work that we give meaning to our existence, we develop our intellect, we learn to face successes and failures, we grow, we fall, and we get up again. And it has so much importance in our lives that we often condition our general wellbeing to the ups and downs of our professional journey.

Sadly, it is easy to observe that a large percentage of people suffer from their work, seeing it as a burden, rather than enjoying it. We just need to walk down the street, take a taxi, enter a public office or work in any type of organization to observe the myriad people who only complain, victimize themselves, lose their motivation and concentration and, logically, lose efficiency in their work and in their lives.

Many people spend more time dreaming about a change than they spend focused on the activities they are performing. However, other people who do the same jobs seem to enjoy it and usually do it with pleasure and excellent disposition. So, I ask you, what is the problem, the job or the person? Sometimes changing jobs could be the solution, but other times that's not possible, or not necessary because is the person (and not the job) that must change. Whether it's one case or the other, if any of this is happening to you, I hope this book can help you understand the problem, find out some ideas for improvement and take proper action.

As part of my final project for my Certification in Positive Psychology, I set up an experimentation group in my office to discuss the relationship between happiness and work. As I had no certainty of the impact or relevance for each person, I decided to gather a group very close to me, trusted people who would allow me to reduce the risk of exposure and could give me honest feedback on this initiative.

I organized a four-hour session that I called "Happiness at Work" where I shared some ideas and exercises to make people reflect on their relationship with their jobs and think about the direction they were imposing to their lives. The reactions were much better than expected, which gave me the confidence to move forward a little bit more.

The first session was followed by a second session, and then a third, and another, and so my message was reaching more and more people within the organization. In those sessions I have seen people laughing, others crying, and even people making relevant decisions about the lives at that very moment, in front of me.

What was that? I'm not sure. Perhaps I managed to open the way for hidden feelings to arise, prompting some people to reflect deeply on their lives and attitudes, encouraging them to take control over their behaviors and choices.

To complement the initial sessions, I started to send out an email every Monday with the idea of reinforcing or complementing some of the concepts discussed in the workshop. Those messages were intending to generate motivation and give a positive boost on how to deal with the work week ahead. Similarly, I first started with my trusted group, the same six people from the initial session, and quickly the distribution list was getting bigger until it was practically out of my control.

The message continued to spread. More people from the organization asked me to be included in the distribution list, then some started sending it to their family and friends outside the organization. Some people changed jobs and took the message with them to their new company giving to my initiative an exponential amplification that, although I am honored, I never aimed.

I started to do this in October of 2016 and I never stopped since then. You can make a simple math to discover how many hundred weekly messages I've sent already. At some point in these years I had the feeling that I didn't have much more to say and I one day I decided to stop, thinking to myself, "make it a good one, this is going to be the last". But fate had its way, and that exact same day, as if a supernatural force had sent him, I received a very encouraging email from a colleague named Flavio who had recently moved to England. Flavio was now working on a very large factory in this new destination and told me that he was sharing my message with a large group of people who awaited it every Monday with enthusiasm because it was very important to all of them. That message gave me the encouragement I needed to keep going.

My weekly emails contain a simple and short message, something to read in less than two minutes, focused on improving the quality of life and giving a positive approach to work, inviting us to observe and improve our behaviors. I often receive replies from different people saying things like "*thank you, this made my day*" or "*this was exactly what I needed today to keep going*" and this is all what I need to feel proud, honored, and happy.

In this book I have compiled some of these messages and linked them with real stories that give shape and life to these learnings, moving them from the abstract to the concrete, to real life, so that I can illustrate them more clearly. All the stories are real. I have changed the names of the characters though to preserve their identity.

Throughout this process of study, experiences, and personal transformation there are four main learnings that I will develop throughout the book:

- **First Learning:** We are owners and accountable for our happiness, through the decisions we take and our own actions.

- **Second Learning:** Life puts obstacles in our way that help us grow and be better. Although they hurt, these "storms" are necessary, among other things, to be able to better appreciate the "sunny days" when everything is calm and peaceful.

- **Third Learning:** Our brain is flexible and manages to change if we work hard and learn how to do it. Therefore, we must stop saying "I am like that" and act to change what we don't like about ourselves.

- **Fourth Learning:** We all have infinite potential. However, not all of us are fortunate enough to discover it, cultivate it properly, and make it flourish. It's our responsibility to discover what our strengths and passions are, so that we achieve maximum performance. It is also our responsibility to encourage others to discover their maximum potential.

These four ideas are developed in the four parts of this book through stories and the compilation of some of these messages that I send every Monday.

I've been asked several times what moved me to write this book. My mission is simple: to help those who may need it, which is closely related to my personal purpose.

I sincerely hope that these stories, learnings, and recommendations help you, inspire you, and encourage you to improve.

Happiness

"Has it ever happened to you that you are looking for an object and it is right in front of your eyes, or you have it in your hand?
Well, something similar happens with happiness. "

The innate and deep desire to be happy is universal across different cultures, genders, ages and races. Being happy is the top priority for most humans. But wait, what is happiness? This is a very difficult question to answer accurately because the meaning of happiness is something very different for each person.

Although there may be levels of general well-being of a population, there is no such thing as measuring individual happiness. Trying to compare the happiness of two people is impossible because it is a unique and individual mental state to which each person gives a different meaning.

Despite happiness being difficult to measure and compare, we still can work to improve it. After all, we are not in a competition to find out who is the happiest person in the world, but instead in a personal challenge to improve our own happiness over time.

Confusing happiness with success is a very common trap. Surveys conducted on young people and teenagers show that almost 80% have as their main aspiration to become millionaires, probably under the assumption that money will bring them all the happiness they need. The media and social networks constantly reinforce this perception, and it is very easy to end up desiring the lives of other people assuming that, behind their glamorous photos and videos, they have a completely happy life.

Multiple studies have shown though that, once basic needs are met, money does not have a direct correlation with happiness, neither fame or popularity because while this looks attractive from afar, the world is full of examples of millionaires and celebrities who commit suicide or end up addicted to alcohol or drugs to tolerate their own lives. On the contrary, there are people who having only just enough for a frugal living, manage to have a happy and fulfilling life.

Contrary to what most people believe, it is not success that leads to happiness. Instead, success and happiness have a reciprocal relationship. Happiness is a state of mind that leads to better relationships, healthier marriages, better jobs, better performance, higher incomes, greater resilience to cope with difficulties, better health, and longevity.

Going further, the correlation between happiness and the events of your life is also very small. I'm sure you know happy people who went through tragic events or suffered accidents, while others with a smooth and easy life spend their lives complaining about everything and may even fall into depression.

In his book "Stumbling on Happiness," psychologist Daniel Gilbert reveals the misconceptions that people have in imagining a future state of happiness as result of the fulfillment of some specific goal. Through his research, he demonstrates that our successes and failures only lead to temporary changes in our level of well-being, as opposed to permanent changes. Hence, achieving a goal such as a graduation, a promotion at work, getting married, or buying a new house, can only temporarily alter our mood, but they do not have the ability to change our general level of well-being and after the ecstasy of the moment we will return to our basal state. Equally, the mood alteration caused by failures is also temporary.

Conditioning happiness to a future event or to some desired position of success presents two problems.

The first problem is never reaching the objective. For example, consider a tennis player whose mindset is that he will only be happy when he manages to be the number one in the ATP ranking. As you can imagine his chances of achieving that goal are tiny, then representing a high risk since he is conditioning his happiness on the fulfillment of that specific target. If he never reaches his goal, he will lose not only the possibility of being happy, but also the opportunity to enjoy every day he has invested in that quest.

By placing happiness "out there", our life is transformed into an unhappy marathon pursuing a goal with the false expectation that we will become happy in the finish line.

The second problem of conditioning our happiness to a future event is presented when we finally reach our so desired goal. Then, we are flooded with an evanescent relief that we confuse with happiness, but it doesn´t last long. If that tennis player happens to become the number one in the world, he of course will feel a relief, great joy and pride, but all of that will be ephemeral and circumstantial. He will soon feel that the achievement is not enough, requiring a new goal, for example, to stay in that position longer than any other tennis player in history, which is the start of a new marathon. And so, we begin to pursue a new goal, even higher, so that we can feel that momentary feeling of (false) happiness again.

In summary, conditioning happiness to future events reduces it to small moments, eliminating the concept of a full happy life. Accepting that vision is to resign ourselves to be unhappy most of the time. Imagine the level of regret a person can feel when, reaching to the end of his life and looking back, can only see a few sporadic moments of happiness and realizes that has not been able to enjoy the journey.

I started this book with the question "Am I Happy?" and one of the things I've learned is that it's not the right question, as it only allows two possible answers: "yes" or "no." The truth is that there is no dividing line indicating that from the line up you are happy and below the line you are unhappy. We all have our moments of joy, sadness and general well-being that are unique, and the secret is to learn how to manage those emotions and the transition between them in a healthy way.

In his book *"Happier",* Tal Ben-Shahar explains *"rather than asking myself whether I am happy or not, a more helpful question is, how can I become happier? This question acknowledges the nature of happiness and the fact that its pursuit is an ongoing process. I am happier today than I was five years ago, and I hope to be happier five years from now than I am today. Being happier is a lifelong pursuit."*

It is important to differentiate between "a good mood" and "happiness". Mood can oscillate throughout the day, but the state of happiness usually doesn't change from time to time, or from day to day, it's not fluctuating.

The mental state of happiness or well-being often does not happen just because, but it takes a constant daily effort to generate and maintain it. That is why, instead of being passive observers, we must take the responsibility of understanding our emotions, being aware of them, and gaining control over our well-being through our actions.

There is a popular phrase that says, *"Happiness is not a destination, it is a journey."* If we think carefully, it makes absolute sense since it is unrealistic to think that one day you will "reach" a place full of happiness that wasn't there the day before and that suddenly invades everything.

The journey to happiness cannot compromise the present. We must enjoy every moment, savoring our life, appreciating and being thankful for everything that we are, and we have. Nothing more, nothing less.

Tal Ben-Shahar suggests that happiness is the reconciliation between pleasure and purpose in our lives. If we manage to feel good in our day-to-day life while we are building something towards the future, we can find that balance. On the other hand, if we only care about the future, we can jeopardize the present by forgetting to enjoy most of our time, while, if we only focus on the enjoyment of the moment, we may be under the risk of feeling empty like we are not building anything important in life.

It is through balanced choices between pleasure (present benefit) and purpose (future benefit) that a person can get a good dose of the desired happiness for longer periods of time. Then we can agree that the secret of having a good relationship with life resides in having a conscious attitude towards the enjoyment of the journey, while building a better future.

PART 1: Manage your 40%

Psychologist Sonja Lyubomirsky in her book "The How of Happiness", developed the formula 50%—10%—40% where through scientific research she and her colleagues argued that approximately 50% of the variation in happiness is determined by genes, and another 10% is determined by the circumstances of our life, such as where we were born or our family environment. This automatically leaves the remaining 40% as the only portion that we can really influence and is under our direct control, basically related to the choices we make every day.

If we all learn to handle that 40% through better decisions, our degree of happiness can increase on a large scale. The challenge is to focus on that 40% rather than spending time worrying and complaining about things we can't change because they're not in our domain. Make no mistake with this number, you are 100% accountable for this portion and this is where you should focus on. The impact of properly managing our 40% is massive if we decide to take full control of our actions in response to our emotions.

To maximize the fraction under our direct control, we need to make decisions aimed at elevating our overall well-being. Some guidelines for this might be found in the answers to the following questions:

Are we clear about our main purpose *in life?*

How do we create free time to invest in the things we most enjoy doing?

Can we determine specific goals so that we can manage our lives instead of others doing it for us?

How can we enjoy more of the time we spend in our work environment?

Do we sufficiently appreciate everything we have or instead spend the day focused on what is missing?

How do we take care of our health and body?

Are we making the best choices regarding the food we eat?

Questions like these were very important for my personal development, and from their answers emerged actions that contributed to my personal well-being, allowing me to take control over my 40%.

Millions of decisions are made throughout life. The important thing is to remember that in every second of our lives we are presented with options, moments where we can decide which path to take. If that process happens consciously, we will have more power over our actions and, consequently, we will be taking care of our own wellness and happiness.

Gratitude

"Gratitude is the single most important ingredient to living a successful and fulfilled life."
Jack Canfield

One of my kids had a very marked tendency to give more importance to the bad things that happened in his life than to the good ones. He was six years old when my wife and I decided to help him to change the way he chose to look at the world.

Every time we asked him how his day had been, almost without exception, he gave a negative or pessimistic response. Without denying that some of the things he said were true, his problem laid mainly in only perceiving the negative facts and ignoring the normal or positive ones. Comments like "the teacher hates me" or "Art class is very boring" were his most common ways of expression.

Our plan was to change his vision of life by inviting him to also observe the good things of every day. It's not about ignoring the bad things, but about balancing them, I explained to him. I proposed that from that night on, before going to sleep, we write down in a notebook the three best things that happened to him during the day and for which he should be grateful. "There aren't three good things every day," he challenged me. "Let's give it a try," I insisted.

With cunning, he suggested that I also write down my three best moments of the day, and that same night we got ready to start the task. With a lot of discipline and perseverance we did this for a few months and the impact was very positive for both of us. Only then I realized that I needed that too.

Over time, we noticed the change as he started to recognize some beauty in his life with more ease. We clearly observed that it is not about great things or extraordinary events. It's about finding extraordinary things in everyday life. The problem is that, despite the beauty is there just waiting to be observed, we normally overlook it.

If there's one thing I've learned about Positive Psychology, it's to stop taking for granted all the wonderful things that life offers me every day. Routinary things, such as getting up in the morning, being able to exercise, feeling the scent of coffee during breakfast, looking out the window and watching the sun brightening the day, or the privilege of having a good job, among many other, are the things that make life worth living. If we do not take the time to observe those things carefully, we can easily overlook them, because our brain is designed to pay attention to negative things, those that are presented as threats, as part of our survival instinct. It takes extra effort to switch our brain off from its natural over-protective mode, so we can better observe, acknowledge, and appreciate the positive and beautiful things in our lives.

There are many things around us every day, every morning, every afternoon, and every night, with the power to make us happy. But we don't pay enough attention to them because we're moving too fast, or we are too absorbed reading the news, or consumed by our mobile phones looking at other people's pictures on social media.

The truth is, not paying attention to these things takes away the opportunity to give them the value they have. If we don't appreciate good things, good things "depreciate", that is, they lose value.

The practice of "Mindfulness" is one of the best tools to enhance the value of all the things we normally take for granted. It is very easy to be mindful. It only requires discipline and effort at the beginning to be able to free our minds from everyday distractions and the usual concerns about the future.

Driven by its main purpose to protect us, the brain is constantly looking to the past, trying to remind us of everything that went wrong, or looking to the future, showing us everything that could go wrong. In its restless obsession to protect us, the present, unless there is an imminent risk, is not something that interests the brain.

To observe the present carefully, we must tell our brain, "STOP! Let me feel this moment". Just stopping consciously to appreciate all the wonderful things around us has a positive impact on how we deal with life. At the same time, if we manage to transform that conscious appreciation into a behavior or action to express gratitude, we can expand that positive impact to others.

In the field of work there are always things (or people) that we don't like, yet we must try to shift our attention towards the things that we enjoy most about work, which are often obscured and hidden behind some other negative things. By observing and appreciating good things carefully, we elevate their importance and allow ourselves to feel grateful for them, balancing in a much better way the negative things that, logically, also exist.

Behavioral Science has extensively researched gratitude as one of the most important drivers of happiness, as it offers a profound impact on multiple aspects of our well-being.

Psychologist Sonja Lyubomirsky explained in a very simple and clear way the most relevant benefits of gratitude:

- Promotes enjoyment of positive life experiences.
- Raises self-esteem.
- Improves recovery from states of stress and trauma by increasing resilience.
- Encourages moral behavior.
- Helps to build and strengthen social connections.
- Inhibits social comparison.
- Decreases negative emotions.

Feeling and expressing gratitude has relevant benefits for your life. Here I detail a few ideas that can help you incorporate it more to your life, to later transform it into a habit or routine:

- **"Thank you" letter**: Write a letter to someone who has helped you. Send it, or even better, personally read it aloud to that person. The effect on that person will be amazing. And the effect on you will be too.

- **Daily Text Messages**: Take your phone and write a thank you message to a person you love or someone who has supported you through tough times. You don't need to explain why, just do it. If someone already came to your head, do it right now.

- **The best part of the day**: This is something that we practice a lot during dinner with my family, talking about the two or three best things that have happened to us during the day. It's usually very simple things, maybe even a good meal or a fun moment.

- **Mindfulness:** This practice can be very effective to better appreciate the present, moving the brain out of its natural way. Even the simplest things like the aroma of coffee or a gesture of kindness can be very rewarding when you pay attention to it.

Purpose

"There is no greater gift you can give or receive than to honor your calling. It's why you were born. And how you become most truly alive."
Oprah Winfrey

One morning, like many others, I arrived at work and met with Andrea, just as we had agreed the afternoon before.

"Hi Andrea, how are you?" I greeted her calmly despite having my head packed with other subjects. Leaving my backpack on a chair, I directly addressed the important subject that we had to discuss.

"I've heard that you want to leave the Company. Let's talk". I sat at my desk facing each other, inviting her to talk.

"Good morning, Pablo. Yes, I've received an offer that I can't reject."

"Well, it all depends on what you're comparing it to. We can also make you an offer to stay" I replied with confidence.

Days before, Juliana, Andrea's boss, had informed me that we'd need to find a replacement for

Andrea because she wanted to leave the company pursuing a new opportunity.

It was hard for me to believe what was happening, as that same week two other people from the same team had also communicated their decision to resign. Those three resignations would have a strong impact on the team, on the business and on my self-esteem. I told Juliana I'd talk to Andrea for convincing her to stay. And there I was, confident I could demonstrate how to execute a retention conversation.

"I don't know, Pablo, I don't think you'll be able to convince me..."

"Let me try," I insisted, refusing to listen to her reasons.

"It's just not a problem with my salary. I've realized I don't like what I'm doing here."

"I understand, that happens, but that also has a solution," I exclaimed. And persevering in my mission I continued, "Let's think of something else you could do here that you might like more."

"I want to be a teacher."

"Teacher?"

"Yes... Teacher. I like to teach, and I like kids. I am a teacher for children with special needs."

"Aha...," I said, and I took a few seconds to find the best approach now that I counted with this new information.

"Andrea, teaching is an honorable job, but I'm sure you already know that the teachers here in Brazil don't make much money. If you make this change, your earnings will decrease significantly".

"Yes, I know"

"And don't you think you can combine the two activities?"

"What do you mean?"

Her question reassured me that there was a possible and beneficial solution for both of us, that she hadn't thought of yet. So, I set out to explain:

"Well, what I mean is that maybe you can keep working here and, a few days a week, you can also teach in your spare time. It would be the best of both worlds for you! Corporate salary while also dedicating time to something you really like to do."

And then Andrea looked at me with such serenity and light that I could feel her words bristle my skin before they came out of her mouth.

"Pablo, I don't think you understand. It's not just that I like to teach, it's bigger than that. When I'm at the front of a class with kids I feel plenty, I feel in my world, an energy springs up that I've never felt here in this office. I feel fulfilled, time flies, I feel that my life gains value, it is a passion that I cannot feel with any other activity."

As I listened to her, I felt a great admiration (almost envy) that she could be so clear about what she wanted to do with her life and was so determined to carry it forward, even despite the financial detriment. I felt terrible trying to convince her not to pursue that.

My eyes filled with tears as I listened to her passionate arguments, so I decided to stop.

"You don't have to continue, Andrea. I apologize, I don't know what I'm trying to do. You're giving me a lesson here. I hope that you will never lose that ability to listen to your heart. And thank you." I said

> *as I got up and gave her a hug. "Let's talk about your replacement."*
>
> *From that day on, I knew I had to do something with my career and my life. Throughout all my subsequent studies in Positive Psychology and my pursuit of happiness at work, I never forgot that conversation. It was a wakeup call that inspired me and prompted me to rethink my purpose in life.*

Multiple studies around the world indicate that more than 50% of people don't feel satisfied with their work. It's terrible to think that more than half of us, while we are working, would rather be somewhere else.

To a large extent, being happy at work is about getting to experience work as a calling, something that contributes to get us closer to our purpose in life.

There is a famous story (possibly a myth) about a cleaning worker at NASA who was asked by, then President of the United States, John F. Kennedy, what his role was, and he said, "I'm helping to bring man to the moon" making it clear that his job was not simply to keep the place clean. He found a greater purpose by linking his daily tasks with the target of the whole organization, allowing him to boost his personal motivation.

Therefore, when you feel that you are doing something that looks repetitive and boring, remember to find in that task, some link that brings you closer to your purpose.

If your main job doesn't fulfill you, it might be a moment to think about starting something new. At the beginning, your job can be your source of capital for you to develop something more aligned to your purpose, until you feel ready to make a complete change. In some cases, this might never happen or might not be possible, then the key will be in managing your time to make your (unavoidable) job compatible with your passions.

Most organizations use the "Position Description" as a tool to organize and distribute work and hire people. In this context, there is little advantage taken of people's passions, since what organizations seek, is someone who fits well with the job description rather than extracting the best from everyone.

It is also true that many people, unclear about their true passions, end up settling with any job that may or may not be related to their calling in life so, after a while, inevitably the dissatisfaction arises. Therefore, it is important to know what our passions and true calling are and constantly effort to be as close to them as possible. I invite you to reflect to discover your calling and work hard to put it into action.

I know all of the above may sound naïve or ungrounded, but the truth is that you have only one life, a finite amount of time, and it makes no sense to spend that time doing something that you dislike or affects you negatively, desperately waiting for the weekend relief. The solution can be as bold as changing to a new job, or at least changing your attitude in front of it. But don't allow yourself to go through life embittered, doing something that makes you unhappy. You have a moral obligation of getting in love with the activities you decide to dedicate your time to.

Goal Setting

"The tragedy of life doesn't lie in not reaching your goal.
The tragedy lies in having no goal to reach."
Benjamin Elijah Mays

Having goals helps us to have a clear destination and allows us to better enjoy the journey as we move forward. It is also a way of communicating what we want to achieve and remind ourselves that we are capable of overcoming obstacles. Lacking goals is like walking without a clear direction where each step creates uncertainty, with the power to lead us to an unwanted place.

Beyond defining our business objectives as we do each year, it is equally important to have and define personal goals, those that will make us a better version of ourselves and progress towards our "ideal self". I'm referring to basic human qualities, like being a better person, augment our strengths, improve our connection with family and friends, elevate our generosity, or contribute more with the society.

Personal goals should help us on having a more integral look of ourselves, helping us in multiple ways, such as enriching relationships with the people we love, being fit and healthy, remedying our finances, organizing better, or simply enjoying life more. According to Dr. Kennon Sheldon of the Department of Psychology Sciences at the University of Missouri, to increase our level of well-being, it is important to express goals in a way that involves growth, connection, and contribution, as opposed to wealth, beauty, and popularity.

An example of goal development dynamics is the technique known as **"SMART"** that refers to five characteristics that our goals must meet. The technique is well known in the corporate world; however, personal objectives can also be written in a "SMART" way.

S	Specific	*"**Calling my mother weekly**" instead of "**Having a better relationship with my mother**"*
M	Measurable	*"**Sign up for the 5 km race in June**" instead of "**Exercise More**"*
A	Attainable	*"**Meditate 15 minutes every day**" instead of "**using all my free time to meditate**"*
R	Relevant	*"**Helping people in need**" instead of "**becoming a millionaire**"*
T	Time Based	*"**Start piano lessons in March**" instead of "**Dedicate time for me**"*

As part of the plan, it is also important to ask ourselves some thought-stimulating questions:

- What aspects of my personality do I want to improve?

- How can I connect more often with my loved ones?
- What are my non-negotiable passions? How can I find time for them?
- What things will I need to set aside to accommodate the things I love and want to do?
- How can I be more connected to my dreams?
- How am I going to contribute more to society, my family, my friends, and my community?

A happy and fulfilling life needs to be integrated by avoiding falling into the trap of measuring personal achievement in a single dimension. On the contrary, success must be measured as a harmonious balance of personal, social, spiritual, physical, financial, and professional improvements. Ultimately, it is up to each individual to determine what success means to them and to strive for their own personal goals and aspirations, rather than simply following societal expectations or examples set by others.

Keep in mind that being rich and famous does not necessarily equate to a fulfilling or meaningful life. Many people who have achieved financial and social success still struggle with problems such as loneliness, addictions, anxiety, and depression. The pursuit of fame and fortune can often come at the cost of personal relationships, mental health, and general well-being.

Don't let the media or peer pressure define success for you. I invite you to make your own definition and express it in the form of goals or objectives, one that instead of wealth and fame (which is restricted to a few), includes ethics, humanity, morality, spirituality, compassion, friendship, loyalty and happiness.

Positivity vs. Negativity

"The more you praise and celebrate your life, the more there is in life to celebrate"
Oprah Winfrey

Popular Cherokee legend:

One afternoon, an old Cherokee explained to his grandson about a battle that happens within people.

"My son, the battle is between two wolves inside us.

One is Negativity. It is anger, envy, jealousy, sorrow, regret, greed, arrogance, self-pity, guilt, resentment, lies, and ego.

The other is Positivity. It is joy, peace, love, hope, serenity, humility, kindness, benevolence, empathy, generosity, truth, compassion and faith."

The grandson thought about it for a minute and then asked his grandfather:

"Which wolf wins?"

The old Cherokee simply replied, "The one you feed."

The way we perceive the world is influenced by our emotions. And depending of the color of those emotions, will be the way we experience our existence in this world.

When we are exposed to positive emotions, we broaden our vision and literally think "out of the box", increasing our possibilities. Being "out of the box" is a metaphor for exemplifying freedom of thought and action, allowing us to be more creative, fostering innovation, variety and exploratory thoughts and actions. Over time, this expanded behavioral catalogue develops new and better skills and resources in us.

Positive emotions promote the increase of an individual's physical, social, intellectual and psychological resources, improving her emotional and physical well-being. This process is cumulative and over time, contributes to making people healthier, better socially integrated, more effective, and resilient. The power to let positive emotions flow provides more access to the pleasures of everyday life.

When positive emotions are scarce or absent, people get stuck, lose freedom, and become painfully predictable.

Negative emotions exist and it is not about suppressing or eliminating them, but instead balancing them properly with the positive ones. Because when the negative dominates, we narrow our vision perceiving mostly the undesirable aspects of life which logically exist, generating reactive, defensive, and possibly aggressive behaviors.

The abundance of negative emotions places us "inside the box", a place where we have no perspective, no clear vision, we do not connect with other people, we isolate and get trapped in our own feelings.

The secret resides in detecting when a negative emotion pushes us "inside the box" and making it a conscious process, we can find a way to get out of that place as quick as possible. There is nothing wrong with getting into the box, in fact, it is inevitable because we all are permanently exposed to negative emotions. But staying in that place is not healthy and impacts our performance.

Negative emotions are generated by thoughts triggered by our brain, in its restless mission to show us all the bad things that may happen. Even though the brain is a super powerful simulator, it is not necessarily accurate. Many of its predictions are incorrect, exaggerated, and fake. The brain is just showing us the worst possible scenario so we can be better prepared to face the catastrophe. However, in the vast majority of the cases the tragic scenario is not going to happen, and we should not allow that unrealistic thought to make us miserable. Remember that the emotion (what you feel) is real, however, the thought that gave rise to that feeling may not be.

Negative emotions increase anxiety and lead to instinctive responses that humans carried from primitive times. Fight or flight could save our lives if a beast was chasing us in the middle of the jungle. And while we are not exposed to as many survival risks today, we often let these instinctive reactions control the simplest situations of everyday life, even acknowledging that there is no logic on that.

Paying more attention to positive emotions (feeding the positive wolf) can help us to balance the adverse facts of life. Also see below some resources that we can use to better neutralize the impact of negative emotions:

- Sleep well.
- Do physical exercise, practice sports.
- Meditate.
- Have free time.
- Practice hobbies.
- Share time with friends.
- Listen to our favorite music.
- Write.
- Reduce the exposure to tragic news.
- Avoid messages of violence or pessimism.
- Avoid toxic people.

The most important that I'd like you to take from this chapter are two things:

1) Many of the negative emotions you feel are generated by fake or incorrect thoughts. It is very important that you detect and eliminate those thoughts quickly.

2) You should make an effort to always have an unbiased view of the world, perceiving both the good and the bad in a balanced way. The effort is needed because your brain will make you pay attention only to the negative.

PART 2: Storms

Without exception, we all go through storms at some point, those moments where the sky is covered with black clouds, darkening the day, preventing us from seeing the sun. When we are in the middle of a storm, it's not easy to stay calm and make good decisions. Those moments bring anxiety, we fear the worst and even simple things are stained with complexity.

I intentionally use the term "storm" to visualize it as a dark and violent event, but still temporary.

Reading an article in a science magazine, I learned that, despite their devastating effects, hurricanes also have some positive effects, such as ending the expansion of bacteria and red tide in the oceans, providing rain to normally arid regions, help balance global warming, replenish matter in coral barriers and spread seeds in remote regions enabling further plant reproduction.

Similarly, storms are necessary in life, among other things to better appreciate the sunny days once they've passed. By hiding the sun for a few hours, storms help us value it more instead of giving it for granted.

The storms of our lives help us give value to all the noble things we have and all the good things that happen to us every day. Because the truth is that every day good things happen to us, only that they lose their value when they become routine, when they become normal, or when they are not a concern. Things as important as our health or the wellbeing of our loved ones are normally ignored when they are ok, and it's only when we've lost them that we pay attention, even becoming the only thing we can think about.

Although it sounds strange, over time I have learned to appreciate and value my own storms, letting the emotions triggered to flow as peacefully as I can manage, and observing them with curiosity, under the full conviction that they will pass soon. What shakes and bothers us like a hurricane today, will fade over time, giving rise again to the blue sky. As time passes, it will be perceived as an event that made us grow and strengthened us to face the next storm even better prepared. The watch-out though is to be careful with the decisions we make during these dark periods since the visibility is normally shortened.

Of course, we don't want bad things to happen, especially because they affect us and other people, but when they happen, we still have options:

1. Complaining, victimizing, giving up, in other words, experiencing it as a catastrophe.

Or...

2. Learn from them, use them to train our patience, our resilience, and our self-control.

In the field of work or business, it is equally presumable that there will be ups and downs and inevitably there will be times of crisis. It's when this happens that our maximum effort, leadership, balanced appraisal, and maturity are required for successfully overcoming the situation, ideally capturing some learnings.

Throughout my career, it is those moments of crisis that I remember more clearly as events driving growth and learning, and where I also was able to appreciate the best demonstrations of solidarity, teamwork, collaboration, creativity, and positive energy.

I don't want a storm to come, but it'll come anyway. What I do want is to be prepared and well balanced to better handle it when the moment comes.

Truth-Lie, Black-White, Pretty-Ugly, Big-Small, Good-Bad, Life-Death. Many words only make sense because their opposite exists. As valuable as we consider the "truth", for example, this word only makes sense because the "lie" exists.

Similarly, there would be no enjoyment of the beautiful things in life if there was no hatred, heartbreak, malice, envy or fear. In other words, storms are a necessary evil for us to value and appreciate, by contrast, the good times in life.

So, when these low moments come to us, we must learn not to lose control, to remain calm and to know that it will be a temporary thing, and its negative relevance will fade over time.

At such times it is very important to gain perspective so we can put the problem in its real dimension. It is very important not to take it as something personal, permanent, and absolute.

- **Don't take it personally:** what happened is not a measure of how good or bad you are. It's something that just happened.

- **Do not take it as something permanent**: the vast majority of crises will not last forever. Even tragic events will be alleviated over time, and we will learn to perceive them with compassion and relief.
- **Don't let it become absolute**: problems are normally restricted only to a specific topics or areas. Don't let them to encompass everything affecting all the aspects of your life.

When we manage to take some distance, we will probably discover that the problem is not big enough to change the course of our lives. In fact, we learn from problems that we had in the past and how we overcame them. Despite having lived them as a crisis and having suffered, today we can look back and see their real dimension. They passed, and we're here, alive, and stronger.

The next storm will pass too. Everything passes.

Watch and stay calm

"Things don't necessarily happen for the best, but once they happen you can make the best out of them."
Tal Ben-Shahar

Talking to a good friend some time ago, I tried to widen his perspective that was blurred by an excess of negative emotions. He was overwhelmed by a conflicting relationship with his boss and the risk of losing his job. He was also going through difficult times with his wife at the point of evaluating a potential separation.

When we go through a situation like the one described above, we are at risk of making bad impulsive decisions, since our frustration, fears, or anxiety reduce our perspective and bias us negatively. Many times, we even doubt of our own strengths, lose confidence and self-esteem as if all that suddenly vanishes.

Although I understood and felt empathy for what my dear friend was going through, I was totally clear that he was not being able to see the full picture. He was just observing all the bad in his life, consequently ignoring many other good things he also had.

These times of crisis are a challenge in our lives and most of the time they consume much of our energy, reaching a point where it is made difficult to think of anything else. We must remember that above the clouds there is always a blue sky. It's always there.

But only when we stop and take a step back is that we can see clearly through the clouds. Instead of fighting the storm it is better to learn to observe our thoughts and feelings calmly, with compassion and curiosity, giving the time for the horizon to be cleared.

Paul Hill, former NASA director, worked on 24 different space shuttle missions as flight director and led the Investigation of the Columbia disaster in 2003. In a recent interview, Hill explained that his teams faced many life-or-death situations, and instead of running like crazy down the halls, they focused on a series of questions.

- What is everything we know and don't know about the situation?
- What does the data really say about the situation?
- What's the worst thing that can happen?
- Do we have enough information to be certain about anything? How can we obtain more information?
- What immediate steps could be taken to continue progressing in the mission and keep everyone safe?

These questions can be of great use in any crisis that we have to solve. I strongly recommend writing them on paper and answering them thoughtfully so that we can organize our thinking and take real dimension of the situation.

Hill closes his interview by saying *"When the crisis breaks out, get a little more information, there's always time to panic later."*

It is also very important to remember that, except for a few professions, most of the problems we face at work are not life or death situations, so pondering them correctly and taking care of them calmly and with good judgment is normally the wisest thing to do.

Stress management

"A year from now, everything you're stressing about today won't even matter."
Anonymous

A few years ago, I was stressed by a very important presentation that we were preparing to receive the visit of the global functional leadership. We were a large team working against the clock to finalize all the details, and the atmosphere was tense.

A person from the team who was very close to me asked me if I was okay since she clearly was able to perceive the tension in me. After digging deeper into the reason for my anxiety, it was interesting to discover that I was approaching the visit as a life-or-death event, as if my life really depended of that presentation. Although it is obvious that the situation was far away from a real danger, unconsciously I was processing it as such. This is usually easier to see in other people rather than in oneself.

Surveys show that 70% of people report experiencing stress every day of their life; and about 20% of people feel extremely stressed to the point where they don't feel they can live a normal life.

Our brain is a very powerful simulator that often projects catastrophic events, causing us to worry deeply. However, 85% of the things we worry about never really materialize. And even when they happen, 80% of the time we manage the situation better than expected. Following that logic, only 3% of the time we worry about things that really have the power to affect us, while in the remaining 97% of times, the situation does not materialize or resolves easily.

Remember this! the brain elaborates catastrophic scenarios because it wants to call your attention, so you are ready for the worst. It does that just for protecting you because that is its main functional mission.

When Dalai Lama was asked what his greatest concern was about humanity, he replied, *"We are so anxious about the future that we do not enjoy the present. Therefore, we do not live in the present or the future. We live as if we are never going to die, and then die having never really lived."*

Stress is a reaction to a situation of change, difficulty or concern about the past or the future. We are all exposed to changes, difficulties, and concerns, therefore we all experience stress. The problem appears when, becoming a permanent condition, this stress doesn't allow us to live a normal life neither thinking with clarity.

Stress is quite common in work environments creating tensions in interpersonal relationships. Employee surveys reveal that excessive pressure for good results and low management quality are the main drivers, and particularly dangerous when both are combined.

The high pressure for good results seems to be successful at first as it moves the organization vigorously, however, extending over time, it can lead to saturation and loss of people's efficiency, increasing turnover.

According to a survey conducted by Randstad US researchers, 60% of employees left their jobs, or are considering quitting because of bad managers. It is remarkable how employees view the company through the lens of their immediate boss. Bosses who mistreat their employees or don't sufficiently appreciate the work they do, create an atmosphere of unnecessary anxiety, leading employees to increase their stress level and resign.

So, if you're a manager, you should know that your mood will affect your entire team. If you're well, calm, and relaxed, your team will be too, and the efficiency will increase. The opposite is logically true as well. Keep in mind that people are not willing to work in a place where culture is toxic enough to destroy their morale. Many times, employees continue to work for these companies, even if they know it is the wrong path, either because they have no choice or because of their ambition and desire to progress.

There is a caveat here. Recent studies have shown that when stress is presented in moderation, is detrimental to health only for people who believe so. Other people instead, that can see it as a way to exercise or get stronger, achieve to have a healthy relationship with stress. In other words, there is a psychological factor that determines the impact of stress on each individual, opening the door to consider two ways to deal with it: as a problem or as a strengthening exercise.

This approach proposes a whole new way of thinking about stress, inviting us to take action towards creating the right conditions for it to manifest in the proper dose and intensity:

1. Impeding stress to become permanent.
2. Not letting it obstruct our view, preventing us from thinking with clarity.
3. Realizing it as a positive thing that, at an appropriate dose, can make us stronger.

Here I share some techniques that I personally find useful and help me control the overall level of stress so that I can experience it as positive stimulus.

Routinary Physical Exercise: increases the production of endorphins, the body's opioid-like natural chemicals that make us feel good. It also reduces blood levels of the stress hormone called cortisol. In addition, it can help clear the mind of thought patterns related to worry and anger. If you are one of those who have the impulse to exercise but change your mind on the go, I recommend the "5-Second Rule": Do you have an impulse to exercise? Go and do it now, avoid a second thought, don't wait, because after 5 seconds your brain will start sending messages to kill the idea.

Laughing and Socializing: Laughter also increases endorphins by reducing tension and cooling stress reactions. It is highly recommended to replace TV or news channels with fun programs or meet up with friends and fun people to laugh more. Loneliness, instead, leads to further increases in morning levels of stress hormone cortisol, poorer immune function, higher blood pressure, and higher chances of depressive thoughts.

Practicing Meditation: It's largely proven that it helps to reduce stress. Meditation contributes to develop "mindfulness", the ability to place all our attention in the present moment, instead of being concerned about the uncertainties of the future. If you have never tried meditation before, I recommend you begin with a guided process. There are plenty of apps for your phone that are excellent to get started.

Volunteering: Devoting time to others, especially people in need, makes you feel plenty and proud, evidencing that you are a generous person, that you have more time available for the good, and more control over your own life. Beyond, helping with your stress, this will also help to increase your self-esteem and wellbeing.

Practicing Hobbies: Especially those that make the time to fly without you noticing, will put your brain to function in a way that will not have resources to continue elucidating scenarios of concern. The brain, despite being an almost perfect machine, has not enough resources to carefully perform multiple tasks simultaneously. So, if you are concentrated doing a puzzle, you will be slowing down the process of permanent elaboration of scenarios. Either music, sports, gardening, painting, photography, dance, writing, or any other discipline (ideally outdoors) works well as long as it's something that you like and fully absorbs you.

Self-fulfilling prophecies

"Whether you think you can, or do you think you can't, in both cases you're right."
Henry Ford.

A few years ago, I witness my own self-fulfilling prophecy when the Director of Resources Humans walked into my office to give me the news that due to a change of plans I had to speak at a conference for the whole office that would take place that same afternoon.

Public speaking was something I certainly did not like and caused me a lot of anxiety. I tried to convince her that was not a great idea, but she insisted until I had no choice but to accept the challenge.

Scared, but with no other alternative, I put myself to work and started to write my speech. Writing was not difficult, however, the visualization of me standing in front of three hundred people was taking me through lot of stress.

I took the stage convinced it wouldn't go well, that I would probably get stuck not being able to continue my presentation, or that maybe someone could ask a question I wouldn't know how to answer. As it is not difficult to imagine, my participation that afternoon was poor and gloomy, certainly I was nowhere near my best version. That day I realized that my negative bias conditioned my performance in a large extent. I was able to confirm I was right about my initial beliefs (I was not good for public speaking), as if confirming my belief was unconsciously more important than my own performance on the stage.

The way in which we predisposed ourselves to do some activity is a very important factor in the result that will be obtained. If we think something will go wrong, we're unconsciously influencing for going wrong. This happens because for most people, being right is very important, it is in fact so important that we prefer to be right rather than performing well. Performing bad allows us to say, "*I knew it...I was right*", making us feel good for our prediction abilities and self-awareness as a compensatory balm for our poor performance.

Similarly, when we wake up thinking "*it will be a bad day*", our attitude during the day can influence our behaviors and the situations around us to make that prediction come true. It is very likely that unconsciously we think and behave conditioned by the negative forecast, in such a way that we ignore positive moments and amplify the negative ones, giving them more importance than they have, expanding their negativity beyond the normal boundaries. Remember that things that you pay attention to, will grow in importance in your head.

In a professional context, this is equally applicable. When a person feels he or she is not qualified for certain position, may not make her best effort, or dedicate enough time to get better, and so her prediction about a mediocre performance will become true. This is called a self-fulfilling prophecy.

The placebo effect is another example of this phenomenon, where patients with some illness experience improvements believing they are taking a medicine when in fact they are just taking a pill with no active drug. That psychological impact, in this case being positive, follows the same logic above.

Reflecting on that experience of public speaking in the story at the beginning of this chapter, helped me to deal with these situations in a healthier and more productive way, with a positive predisposition, higher self-esteem, lower personal judgment, and better results, coupled with the ability to capitalize my experiences into learnings.

Just as there are negative self-fulfilling prophecies (I think it will go wrong-it goes wrong-"I was right"), there are also positive cycles (I think it will go well-it goes well-"I was right").

In the positive cycle described above (I think it will go well-it goes well-"I was right"), a bad result could also happen, but even in that case, the person will try to find the root cause of the failure and how she can improve, with a growth mindset that will lead to continuous improvement, expecting to be right in the next opportunity.

A manager has a great influence on the success of their team by handling these positive and negative expectations. One of their main responsibilities is to keep the team motivated and focused, where each person understands what is expected and feels able to deliver accordingly, so managers must work on the insecurities and make their best effort to eliminate them.

These insecurities present in two types:

- Self-insecurities of the people in the team. This type needs to be worked with positive coaching, guiding and cheering for those in the team that need to trust more in their own performance.

- The insecurities that the manager has about a member of the team. When this happens, the manager unconsciously conveys that insecurity to the team influencing the overall performance. Under the same logic, if the manager expects great things and manifests it with conviction, will be giving a great message of trust, creating the right conditions for them to perform at their highest level.

Despite being very powerful, the human brain struggles when pre-existing beliefs and reality are not aligned. This phenomenon is known as "cognitive dissonance" and our brain needs to resolve such a discrepancy quickly.

It is normal to observe a manager who convinced that certain person is the "best" employee in his team and compliments all her work with a positive bias, ignoring or minimizing her faults and giving greater relevance to the accomplishments. Similarly, if the boss thinks an employee is not a good performer, he will see everything with a negative lens and find all the bad things in the work of that person.

In the example above, the manager has no good or bad intentions, this is simply how our brains work, making an unconscious effort to reconcile pre-existing beliefs with current reality, not being able to tolerate the inconsistency.

If such a mismatch still exists, our brain may take one of these two paths:

1. Modifies the original belief: *"maybe John is not as bad as I thought",* re-labeling him as one of the "good performers".

2. It removes the evidence: "*He did well this time, but it's probably just an exception, he was lucky or maybe someone helped him*", keeping the original belief with no change.

This happens basically because our appreciation of the reality is never pure. When we observe an event, we are capturing what is actually happening through our five senses (what we can see, hear, smell, touch or taste), but this is filtered through our pre-existent beliefs, our conditioning fears, experiences from the past, etc. Therefore, the same exact event can be perceived in a totally different way by two different people.

Self-Fulfilling Prophecies are supported by the theory of the Cognitive Dissonance. When you think something won't work well, you're preparing your brain to fail, and you increase your likelihood of a Self-fulfilling Prophecy because the brain will make a huge effort to avoid a cognitive dissonance trying to prove that beliefs and reality are aligned. Hence, it will likely play against your performance to demonstrate its assertiveness.

So, knowing the theory, it would be very good to use it in our favor to generate positive expectations so we can create a Positive Self-Fulfilling Prophecy.

According to the quote in the header of this chapter, Henry Ford already knew about this theory one hundred years ago, yet we continue to fall into the same traps.

I want to emphasize that under no circumstances should we use this theory to be off guard and let optimism prevent us from seeing reality. Understanding the risk of a situation and properly preparing us for a contingency is a correct and prudent behavior. Yet, even working with contingency plans, we can still have an intentional positive inclination for success.

PART 3: Personal Change

We are not machines. In front of the same stimulus, every person reacts in a different way.

Have you ever wondered why? It turns out that our brain is made up of billions of neurons that communicate with each other by releasing chemicals called neurotransmitters (e.g., dopamine and glutamate), into the space between them known as synapses. It is a perfectly coordinated system that regulates demand and response, controlling the "turn" of each neurotransmitter. In the face of a stimulus, there is a set of neurons that fire simultaneously creating a neural circuit. Over time these circuits are strengthened and become more robust and automatic as a result of our experiences and our education, to the point where they are transformed into habits. For example, if you drive and see a red light, your right foot will automatically stop accelerating and move to the brake pedal. This process is practically automatic and does not require reasoning or planning, as our neurons can direct the movement of our foot based on a visual stimulus.

Our emotions, actions and reactions are also determined by this giant complexity of neural circuits that make us unique. Contrary to what was believed twenty years ago, our brain has the ability to change and modify these neural circuits if we learn how to do it. The recent development of brain scanning technologies, were able to prove the brain is a plastic organ that can change its own structure and function, even in old age.

Neuroplasticity is arguably the most important advance in neuroscience since scientists first sketched the basic anatomy of the brain. This revolutionary discovery promises to overthrow the centuries-old notion that the brain is rigid and immutable like a machine or that it is wired like a computer.

This topic is very complex for the interests of this book, but if you find this is something of your interest, I recommend reading Norman Doidge's book "The Brain That Changes Itself" that describes with mastery a lot of medical cases and examples of how these discoveries can change the lives of many people.

I had never paid attention before until I started to read more about neuroplasticity, and then I felt curious at the beginning and then empowered when discovered that I was able to modify my own neural circuits. So, I set out to experiment how to change some things I didn't like about me.

I'll explain this with an example. I've always been very impatient while driving my car. I was one of those people who got irritated if the driver in front didn't start immediately when the traffic light went green or getting anxious in traffic jams. When I was living in Sao Paulo, I spent many hours every day in the very busy and unpredictable traffic, which had a very negative impact for me, so I decided to work on this as my first change experiment.

What did I do? First, creating a ritual of repetition. I wrote the following sentence on a piece of paper: *"I'm patient, even when I think I'm wasting my time, and enjoy*

PART 3: Personal Change   65

every moment of my life." And I set the routine to spend a few seconds to read it aloud every morning when I woke up. I also stuck a post-it® on the dashboard of my car.

Second, handling my impulses and forcing my behaviors at the beginning. Remember the subject of cognitive dissonance? The brain needs beliefs and behaviors to be aligned, so sometimes behaviors must be forced for the brain to "believe it." As I found myself sitting in traffic and started to feel irritated and nervous, I made a huge effort to stay calm and drew a smile in my mouth repeating the phrase *"I am patient, even when I think I am wasting my time, and enjoy every moment of my life."* I began to change my actions and perceptions, looking out the window of my car, discovering things I had never observed, beautiful houses, parks, people, trees. In addition, using mobile internet, I started listening to a very fun radio program from Argentina that made me laugh a lot, determined to make that moment in traffic into something positive.

Third, repeating the two previous steps with great perseverance to create the habit. According to Dr. Pascual Alvaro Leone, neurology advocate at Harvard Medical School, it takes six months to create a new neural circuit and about ten months to make it permanent. It's only through consistent repetition that we achieve to create new permanent neural pathways.

I started to see changes and managed to improve. I'd be lying if I say that now I enjoy getting stuck in traffic, yet I can go through that experience nowadays without being angry or allowing it to affect my mood. In addition to working on my patience, I also worked on improving other aspects of my personality, such as my extremely high expectations and self-demand, my frustration in front of adversity, my resilience, my kindness to other people, and a few other things.

My improvement journey is really not important here. What I want you to take away from the story is the conviction that if there's something about you that you don't like, you shouldn't settle for a simple "I am like that." Don't be "like that" if you don't like it. Change!

In this section of the book, I will tell you about some actions that helped me improve my personal and professional life, hoping that they can also help you.

The right question: How would you like to be?

"When we let our own light shine, we unconsciously give other people permission to do the same"
Nelson Mandela

> *Once, a young man in his thirties, looking impeccable, came to my office for a job interview, his hair was properly styled, perfectly shaved, and he was wearing an outfit of sophisticated appearance. After a few minutes of conversation, I asked him to tell me a little about him and his aspirations.*
>
> *"My aspiration is to become a CEO or a functional VP over the next 5 years," he replied immediately, clearly excited and sitting on the edge of the chair.*
>
> *"Great! Ambitious aspirations, good. Tell me about yourself."*
>
> *"I studied Administration in the United States and also an MBA. I started my career..."*
>
> *For 15 minutes I listened carefully to his short but remarkable trajectory*
>
> *"Very impressive— I congratulated him but suspected that his excessive ambition might play against him."*
>
> *"I'd like to hear more about things that aren't on your resume, like your aspirations as a person."*

> *The guy stared at me as if he was paused. I noticed his discomfort.*
>
> *"Well, like I said, my aspirations as a person are to be CEO or VP...", he insisted.*
>
> *"Sure, but those are still professional aspirations. I'm asking about **personal** aspirations."*
>
> *"What you're telling me is WHAT you want to be, and that's fine, it's clear. Now, what I'm asking you is HOW you want to be. Would you like to be more generous? Kinder? Better team player? Mentor?"*
>
> *Despite his difficulty in understanding the relationship between that question and the role he was applying for, the conversation continued kindly for another 30 minutes and while I intended to take him to that soft side, he desperately tried to return the conversation to the position and his professional aspirations.*
>
> *"I'm graduated from one of the best Colleges in the world and I want to grow. My dedication is a hundred percent focused on work."*
>
> *After one hour of conversation, we finished the interview, and I was left wondering how this smart guy would fit into the team, because in addition to worrying about his technical skills I had to make sure he shared the values and culture of the organization.*
>
> *I decided to keep thinking about this candidate and what I needed for my team before offering him the role.*

How do you want to be? We spend a lot of time defining **what** we want to be in the future, which is expressed mainly as an economic position, status, career hierarchy, profession or title.

However, we rarely take on the job of reflecting about **how** we want to be, meaning the qualities of our personality that we like, and those that we do not like and prefer to change. Our character and personality are the main factors why our true friends love us, respect us, and value us. And you know, if someone is your friend because of your money, status, or titles, then that is not a true friend.

Focusing on the "what", may be effective in the short term, but certainly insufficient. It will end up leading us to a situation of physical and spiritual loneliness if we do not complement it with the development of our qualities as a person.

A very powerful exercise that I've learned and applied is the "ideal self". It is a deep reflection to define how you would like to be, and the work needed to get closer to it.

The first thing you need to do is to write on a piece of paper what are those characteristics that you would like to demonstrate more often. Do you want to be more generous, more fair, less arrogant? Also write down the reason for that desire. What bothers you today? This is important so you can find a reason for your effort.

Then, you can move to "action mode" and start by creating a ritual, as I explained in the Personal Change introduction. Through the ritual you will create a routine of reading and repeating your "ideal self" every day, as many times as possible. Place reminders in as many places as you can: in the bathroom, in your car, in your fridge, etc. Work with one or two changes at a time so you can be focused and stay consistent.

Along with the repetition ritual, you must start acting in alignment with the desired change, even if it's a little forced at the beginning, because you need to re-educate your brain, and for that your acts and your thinking need to be aligned. If you say "I'm humble" you must act humbly, and your brain will gradually begin to control the impulses of arrogance.

You must repeat this for months for it to become a new solid neural circuit if you want the change to last. While difficult at first, it becomes easy after a few days, almost natural when done consistently for a few weeks, and automatic over about six months.

Although this may sound like a game, by doing this procedure over and over, you will be re-educating your brain, weakening your existing neural circuits, and replacing them with brand new circuits. In other words, you'd be provoking a physical change in your own brain. If you have perseverance, that change will sustain, becoming a new habit.

There is no risk in trying and enjoying the experience.

Your best version

"Your ultimate goal in life is to become the best version of yourself. Your immediate goal is to get on the path that will lead you there"
David Viscott

One morning, Fernando, a person from my team, arrived late to a team meeting with an uncommon but visible bad mood. Along the whole hour, he seemed to be a mix of absent and upset. He over-reacted when one of the team members made a minor observation about the work of a member of his team.

At the end of the meeting, I asked him to stay a few minutes to better understand what was going on. We had lunch together that day he disclosed that he was going through a bad time in his personal life. With empathy for his problems, I made my best effort for him to reflect about his behavior during the meeting. "You are an influential person in the team. When you are well, you spread a very positive energy", I wanted to acknowledge him, "but be careful Fer, that when you are not well you also pass it forward"

We all have ups and downs, times when we feel better and we shine, and other moments when we get caught up by our own unhelpful emotions.

Emotions are neither good nor bad. What we feel is what we feel and that is real. We all go hundreds of times every single day through a mix of positive and negative emotions, sometimes changing from one to the other in seconds, driven by unadvertised triggers. Sometimes, a simple visual image or a sound, can change our humor in seconds.

The problem arises when we allow those emotions to control our behaviors. And the invitation is to manage in a more conscious and healthy way the power that we give to these emotions for conditioning our behaviors.

Even if you don't want to, when you misbehave as a result of a negative emotion, you're automatically expanding the negative wave to others. Behaviors are highly contagious, both for the good and for the bad.

It is important to learn how to breathe…. a long breathe so we can turn the impulse of a negative behavior into a positive one, escaping from the emotional trap. We must learn to break the chain "emotion-reaction" replacing it by a healthier chain "emotion-reflection-action", by identifying what was the trigger that made us feel bad, gaining perspective, give that emotion its right place and dimension, and chose our best possible conscious action.

A domestic problem doesn't excuse us for talking rudely to a person in our work environment. Likewise, a work problem should not lead to reactive behaviors towards our family. If something like this happens to you one day and you think about it for a few moments, you'll surely recognize that it is not even close to your real intentions.

No one can question your right to be angry, sad or distressed, however, you are one hundred percent responsible for your behaviors and you have no right to spread your bad mood.

When you display your best version and behave as such, you feel free, calm, think more clearly and you are also automatically inviting other people to do the same, creating a more positive and favorable environment for everyone.

Mastering the ability to understand your emotions and manage your behaviors is an attribute of maturity that will allow your loved ones, your work colleagues, and yourself to always enjoy your best version.

Time management

"Until we can manage time, we can manage nothing else."
Peter Drucker

In a conversation with a work colleague, a few years back, she shared with me that was feeling totally overwhelmed by her duties, in such a way that time never seemed to be enough.

She was trying to cope with all the obligations of being mother, wife and a corporate executive and how difficult was to find a balance with all that. While she was trying to do so many things including working, cooking, taking care of the house, driving her kids to school, and eventually working out, her feeling was that she was not dedicating enough time to any of that.

The cherry on the top for her frustration was that, given her current time management struggle, she had been postponing some other activities that she classified as personal passions. As I asked her to tell me more, she described her passion about music and her dream about playing an instrument one day. It was not in her near future plans though, as she didn't want to put more things in her already overloaded agenda.

Then, I remembered an exercise that I learned before and proposed her to experiment with that. "It's very simple", I explained, "it invites to think about yourself as an anonymous person. It's about imagining for a moment that nobody will know anything about you, neither your success or failures, nor if you are rich or poor and most important, nobody would have any expectations about what you do or you don't do". So, I asked the obvious question, "Under such conditions, what would you do with your time?"

Her answer was predictable but important since it allowed her to see that some of the activities she was filling her life with, were externally driven and she wouldn't do many of them in the context of being anonymous. "You must find a way to include time for music in your life"

Having time is much more important for happiness than having material wealth. Think about it, as stated earlier, 50% of our happiness is genetically determined, another 10% is given by the circumstances of life and only the remaining 40% is the portion under our control. The way you use your time is the most determining factor for that 40%. Life is nothing more than a combination of time and energy and it's you (and only you!) who determine how to use those two resources. The clock ticks the same for all of us.

Having time to do the things we like is taking control of our lives. However, we love to say that we are busy, really busy. Saying we are busy seems to be one of the main ways we let people know that we are important, as we have been brought up to believe that if we are busy, we are important. But think about it for a moment, the lack of time to talk, socialize, exercise, play or love doesn't make us important, it makes us miserably unhappy instead.

Either in your work or in your personal life, when you find yourself apologizing to someone because you couldn't make the time to get to know them, answer a call, reply to a message, or simply acknowledge their existence because you have been "very busy", consider the REAL messages you are sending to that person:

- *My time is more important than yours.*
- *I'm not very good at prioritizing my time.*
- *I want you to judge me based on how busy I am, not how productive I am.*
- *You're not a priority, or at least that thing you want to discuss with me is not a priority for me.*

If this describes something that has been happening in your life, I encourage you to reconsider your priorities and invest quality time to the people and activities you love. Having time to invest in the really important things is a fundamental contribution to the overall well-being of every individual.

Meeting your goals

"Review your goals twice every day in order to be focused on achieving them. "
Les Brown

As I explained in a previous chapter, it is important to have clear goals both for the professional and personal life. Goals help us to have clarity about what we want to achieve and to know where we are heading. The simple fact of knowing that your target is North, provides orientation and serenity while walking northbound, even if you don't have precision about the exact final destination yet.

Once the objectives are defined, it is important to have discipline and routine management to make sure that we are moving consistently towards achieving them. Many times, the urgent matters beat the important things and we soon realize we've gone a month without having advanced in our goals.

Many years ago, during my first years of career, getting to the end of a very intense month-closing week, my boss came to my desk inquiring about my progress towards my annual goals in the last few weeks.

I remember how bad I felt because we both knew that I'd been firefighting, answering emails, sending reports, and so on, and all my energy got consumed by operational issues that were not relevant contributors to my annual goals.

Distraction and excuses exist in abundance leading us to derail from our goals. The antidotes are discipline, routine and concentration.

These simple tips that I list below can help to keep you on track towards meeting the long-term goals.

- Outline the activities and tasks that are responsible for successfully meeting your goals. Don't stay only with the long-term goal statements and instead set intermediate milestones. For example, if your goal is to run a 10k race and you are not a frequent runner, you can propose yourself to run 1k in the first month, then 2k in the second month and keep growing as you move. If you only focus on the final goal, you can get easily frustrated finding it's too difficult or too far away.
- Define daily activities (aligned with big long-term goals) that take you to deliver the milestones. Write this down before starting each day, ideally the night before, being as specific as possible. This is about creating routines and consistency to drive habits that move you a little bit every day towards your goals. Writing a book is a difficult task for most people but if you write one page every day, after a few months, you can have one finished.
- Minimize the permanent interruptions that break the flow of your concentration, pulling you away from your priorities.

This last point is of extreme importance, especially in the times we live, and it's specifically related to the mobile phones. Smart phones are a technological jewel, and I still don't understand how we could survive without them. I like my phone very much and helps me to be more efficient, faster, communicate with my family when I travel or having a video call with my parents, brothers and friends that live far way. However, it's a non-stop source of distraction that come in the form of text messages, calls, emails, news, twits, social media, etc, etc, etc. While with a simple click we now have access to things that were impossible before, we are at risk of spending way too many hours surfing randomly, purposeless, and without progress.

Today's workplace also encourages lack of concentration (opposed to mindfulness), as there are multiple matters competing all the time for our attention, generating distraction, loss of efficiency, and disconnection with our main goals.

The contrary to the above description happens when we are focused, experiencing a full connection with the activity we are performing, with no room for distractions. This is when track of time disappears, and the hours seem to pass in minutes. Have you ever experienced that time flies when you read a book you like, or when you cook, play a sport, or just talk to a friend? We can create this same idea of full connection at work, leading to higher performance and better results.

Some tips to promote a full connection:

- Reduce the use of text messages or any messaging apps: the vast majority of messages can wait to be answered.
- Respond to emails and messages at specially assigned times of the day and block them when concentration is needed.

- Eliminate the "Desktop Pop-Up Alert" in the email settings.
- Close the email program in your computer when working on a presentation or when attending a meeting, no matter whether the meeting is face-to-face or virtual.

Help Others

"Rivers don't drink their own water. Trees don't eat their own fruit. Sun doesn't give heat for itself. Flowers don't spread fragrance for themselves. Living for others is the rule of nature. And therein lies the secret of life."
Amit Gupta

In the summer of 2019, Gaby, my wife, proposed to me to do an activity with our children to revitalize in all of us two fundamental qualities such as Generosity and Gratitude. She is very passionate about the study of "Character Strengths" and all the time organizes family initiatives to observe and develop our personality strengths so we can discover which are the ones that naturally emerge from us, as well as stimulate those that need a little more effort. We would take advantage of the visit of my dear sister in law and her family, who visited us in Chicago, to share this activity with them as well.

It was a volunteering activity in a Non-profit organization called "Feed My Starving Children," that is supported only by donations and has the mission to deliver a nutritional meal to children in need in dozens of countries around the world. Millions of children are helped by FMSC meals every day. It was a beautiful experience that filled us all with incredible energy and excitement and I was so positively impacted that decided to continue going there every single week after that first time.

Every Saturday morning I go to FMSC to participate in a two-hour activity, and while we pack the food and produce the finished meal boxes, my soul fills with joy. About 150 people organized into several groups participate in each session. The first ten minutes take place in the induction room where the activity is explained in detail and the coordinator specifies the final destination for the meals produced that day. Then the packing operation begins for almost ninety minutes and at the end of the session, it is reported back to all participants how many boxes have been processed. They nicely express that, not in how many cases were produced but instead saying something like *"with what we made in this session we will be able to feed 200 children for a year"*. I love that part so much! After many months doing the same thing I still can't leave that place without some tears in my eyes. When I come home after that activity, I feel plenty, in peace, and energized.

I decided to interview Kristie, a supervisor at FMSC so I could better understand that energy I feel.

"Kristie, how does it feel to work here?"

"I started here only 7 months ago after I worked my whole life in a corporation. This is fantastic. Here we work with a lot of companionship, we are all a great team and we are very clear about our mission. It's really a very strong feeling when you realize that the job here is to save lives. We worked for children who would otherwise die from lack of food."

> *"How would you say this work differs from others you've had before?"*
>
> *"There is no one here concerned about climbing positions or competing with other people. This work extracts the best from everyone."*
>
> *"And why do you think that is achieved?"*
>
> *"Because this place depends 100% on donors and volunteers, everything is born from the heart. And because there's no profit intention, everything is easier. Here come children, adults, and the elderly, all with the same intention of helping and giving their best. And everyone, without exception, leaves here with a smile and a heart full of joy. Here we, the staff, feel important, and in the same way, every person who comes to help feels important."*
>
> *"Do you feel that this job has changed your life?"*
>
> *"Absolutely. I am 53 years old and for the first time in my life I love my job and I enjoy going to work. It doesn't really feel like a job. As my husband says, 'every day is a celebration when you work here'".*
>
> *"To what extent would you say this work is aligned with your purpose in life?"*
>
> *"It's very much aligned. This work helps me to be who I want to be: a person with a service purpose. Helping other people is what moves me and that's why I'm so proud to work here. Once you come to work here you can no longer leave, you need it to fill your heart. Helping others is in our nature as human beings and doing so is what gives us meaning and fulfillment in life."*
>
> *"Thank you, Kristie!"*

Let us imagine for a moment the strength and results that could be achieved if that same energy and passion that

Kristie has could exist in every work environment every day.

If you don't have the fortune of working in a place like FMSC, you still can contribute to the society in many other different ways. Some of the questions below are intended to invite you to reflect about that:

- Can I identify an altruistic purpose within my organization?
- How can I help my company to support more volunteering activities?
- How can I spend more time helping others within my workspace?
- Can I help other people improve in their career?
- If I don't find any of this inside my work, what can I do outside to make a contribution to the world?

Helping others generates a real sense of pleasure, excitement and well-being, making us feel more connected to the world, increasing our self-esteem and giving us a high level of personal satisfaction.

Multiple studies have shown that people with altruist behaviors in the workplace, are more likely to feel happier and more satisfied with their jobs. Simple acts of kindness, expressions of gratitude, and the offer of support to colleagues can make us feel much better about ourselves while improving the work environment.

Giving is a way to demonstrate our love, compassion, appreciation, gratefulness, or admiration towards another person. When our offer is authentic, it doesn't need to be compensated in any physical way because the main return is to feel good with ourselves, to feel better human beings, and more satisfied with our lives. In other words, the person giving or helping, is the one obtaining the largest benefit, thus there is no other reward needed.

Life takes on its most extraordinary dimension when used to help others to grow and flourish.

Lead the change

"Be the change you want to see in the world"
Gandhi

> *There's a story about a mother who brought her six-year-old son to Mahatma Gandhi's house. When her turn came, after several hours of queuing, she asked him:*
>
> *"I beg you, Mahatma, tell my son not to eat any more sugar. He's diabetic and he risks his life by doing it. He doesn't listen to me anymore, and I suffer for him."*
>
> *Gandhi reflected and said:*
>
> *"Sorry ma'am, I can't do it now. Bring your child in two weeks"*
>
> *Surprised, the woman thanked him and promised to return as he had asked. Fifteen days later, she returned with her son. Gandhi looked the boy in the eye creating a great connection and indicated:*
>
> *"Child, you must stop eating sugar."*
>
> *Grateful, but confused, the mother asked:*
>
> *"Why did you ask me to bring him two weeks later? You could have told him the same thing the first time we came."*
>
> *Gandhi replied: Fifteen days ago, I was eating a lot of sugar, too.*

Integrity is the hallmark of great leaders, and this attribute becomes visible when they lead by example. Such as Gandhi was not able to recommend something he was not doing, managers who wants collaboration in their organization must collaborate, and if they want respect in the work environment, they must show respect to others. In a nutshell: They must be the change.

This idea of leading by example of course should apply to all areas of life and especially in the education of our children. If we want our children to work hard and be generous, we must work hard and act generously.

How to start putting this idea into action?

Make a list of the values you'd like to see in your workplace.

- Want to see more kindness?
- Want to see more humility?
- Want to see more transparency?

Write down the values that are important to you. Then make a personal commitment to exemplify them in the office. For example, if you want a more positive environment, act positively.

Lead Your Own Emotional State.

William James (1842–1910) was one of the most important psychologists and philosophers in the United States of Harvard Medical School, also known as the "Father of American Psychology". He said, *"I don't sing because I'm happy, I'm happy because I sing."*

The misconception is that we should first be happy for then act accordingly, but James insisted on the idea of trying otherwise, for example, acting as if we were happy until we really feel it. Just as feelings condition our behaviors, the opposite is also true. By forcing behaviors, we get them to impact on how we feel.

The first step is to clearly understand what is under our direct control, and what is not.

Out of our control

1. What other people do.
2. What other people think.
3. What other people say.
4. The judgment and reactions of others.

Under our control

1. Our mood.
2. Our actions and behaviors.
3. Our motivation and team spirit.
4. Our ideas and beliefs.

Focusing on what we can control is mastering our ability to influence our life. On the contrary, putting our attention on things outside of our control, drains our energy, exhaust us, and leads to frustration. The challenge is to free up our mind from what we don't control and let it just be.

A big part of the human misery and frustrations is generated by situations that don't result as we expect. It is not about the situation itself being good or bad, but simply different to the expectation.

When the result is under our control, logically makes sense to do our maximum effort so we can be on track towards the expected results. But many times, it's just external drivers that determine the reality, and even if it's very different to our expectation, it makes no sense to suffer for it. The reality is what it is, either we like it or not, and when there is no action plan that can solve the situation, it doesn't worth to suffer.

The attention must be always put on observing the situation, understanding how our emotions are affecting our mood, and logically how to choose our best possible behavior, one that contributes to elevate our spirit and the spirit of all the people around us. It requires maturity to take distance, think, distinguish things inside and outside our control zone and take the right action when appropriate.

Taking accountability for our emotions and behaviors is of paramount importance and the best we can do for taking control of our mood and consequently of our wellbeing. We must never forget that in every moment of life, no matter how complicated the situation may present, we have choices, and it is our duty to use them wisely.

Personal Impact

"Act as if what you do makes a difference. It does."
William James

Some time ago I read this story by Loren Eiseley

> *"There was a human boy walking along a beach. There had just been a storm, and starfish had been scattered along the sands. The boy knew the fish would die, so he began returning them to the sea. But every time he threw a starfish, another would wash ashore.*
>
> *An old man happened along and saw what the child was doing. He called out, 'Boy, what are you doing?'*
>
> *'Saving the starfish!' replied the boy.*
>
> *'But your attempts are useless, child! Every time you save one, another one returns, often the same one! You can't save them all, so why bother trying? Why does it matter, anyway?' called the old man.*
>
> *The boy thought about this for a while, a starfish in his hand; he answered,*
>
> *'Well, it matters to this one.' And then he flung the starfish into the welcoming sea."*

Our actions can easily look irrelevant in comparison to the suffering of humanity. But if we all think that way, then nobody would be helping other people, making the world a terrible place to live. The importance resides in doing something good for someone else, no matter if you are helping only one person. Then, if you can help two people, it's even better and if life offers you the chance to help a hundred, go for it!

Let me tell you a story. I had the privilege of travel to Vietnam along with other colleagues from my company as we had been selected to participate in a leadership training. Targeting to develop new skills to work and behave under pressure, we were purposely assigned extremely ambitious goals to meet during that week.

In Vietnam, a third of children under the age of 5 suffer from nutrition problems especially in rural areas. Our goal was to generate ideas to create changes in the nutritional profile and eating habits of that population by helping some Non-Profit organizations that had already been working on the issue for years.

Most of my colleagues seemed engaged and excited but two or three days after the kick-off I started to feel a decrease in my energy and motivation. I started to predict that we would be wasting our time there. The goal (as my brain processed it) looked totally unreachable and out of our control. I knew that even if we were able to develop a few proposals, they would be insignificant. The government agents and members of supporting organizations we met talked about more than 80 million people dealing with this problem under extreme poverty conditions. The nutritional deficit was the result of a strong legacy of farmers that have been cultivating and eating only rice for several hundred years. How could we change that in a week of work? That was certainly impossible.

We had a noble goal and a team of extremely capable people; however, everything was very complicated. Meetings with the local organizations were not clear, and communication was not flowing properly. We were barely able to communicate with government officials in a very basic English or sometimes through translators.

Despite our efforts, most of the week had passed and we had only one day left to close the proposal and present it. Even though we developed a few great ideas, I was discouraged and troubled because, I knew they weren't enough to make a real impact, and even less to make it sustainable.

I couldn't sleep that night due to the anxiety of the last day along with the brutal jetlag. As I tossed and turned in my bed, the memory of the starfish's tale on the sand came to mind. Remembering that story reconciled me with the cause and the sleep, and the next morning I could see our work with different eyes. I stopped thinking about the millions I wouldn't be able to help and began focusing on the hundreds I could.

It was a wonderful week and a huge privilege to have that experience. Although logically the nutritional problem in Vietnam was beyond our reach, I know that the work we carried out that week has at least improved the lives of a few people. Realizing that every small contribution helps, allowed me to return happily to my home with a comforting feeling of accomplishment.

The world is full of big problems and sometimes we just don't do anything about it because we think we won't make an impact. It's a mistake to underestimate the effect of our actions, no matter how small they may seem to be. That is a trap that intimidates and paralyzes us. If we instead focus on helping someone, it's quite likely that we can evidence the impact, and the impact is usually exponential because, unconsciously, we are inviting that person to pass it forward, and do the same for someone else.

PART 4: Your Potential

"The potential for greatness lives within each of us."
Wilma Rudolph

In his book "Frames of Mind" (1983), Harvard psychologist Howard Gardner wrote that we need to stop asking *"How smart is this student?"* and start asking *"How is this student smart?"*

This new question then assumes that everyone is smart, and that we are intelligent in different ways, with different strengths.

Gardner explains that there are seven different types of intelligence and that we all have a different and unique composition of them:

Linguistic intelligence. It is related to the use of words, so the most important capabilities are effective writing, reading, and a good memory.

Logical-mathematical intelligence. This focuses on problem solving, reasoning, recognizing patterns, and the ability to think conceptually about numbers.

Spatial or visual intelligence. This focuses on solving spatial problems, for things like playing checkers, for which a spatial vision is needed, or the mental representation of accurate images. This type of intelligence is usually found in artists, designers, or architects.

Musical intelligence. It is the one needed to interact with instruments and to recognize and analyze sounds.

Body or kinesthetic intelligence. It is the one that deals with body movements to express emotions, compete, or create. Its focus is on the precision and control of the different parts of the body.

Intrapersonal intelligence. This intelligence is the most intimate because it is focused on self-knowledge. A person with intrapersonal intelligence, normally possesses good self-esteem and highly aspirational personal projects.

Interpersonal intelligence. It has a direct connection to empathy towards others and makes it possible for people to socialize and work together for identifying and overcoming problems.

Gardner proposes that we are all intelligent and that the improvement of one or several of these types of intelligence depend on the extent to which we developed them or not.1

The role of leaders is to help people identify their strengths, encouraging them to use those more often, to extract the maximum possible benefit. When we talk about a person's potential, we must ask ourselves, *"potential for what?"* Remember that potential is a very wide concept. For example, questions like *"what makes this person remarkable?"* or *"What are their talents or gifts?"* are more adequate and precise.

PART 4: Your Potential

An individual's potential is an ability, not yet developed, that will allow them to get the most out of their life. The most important is that the capability exists, it is a possibility, a talent, even if has not yet been developed. It's everything a person can achieve.

We are all able to do things like no one else can do because we possess a singular combination of capacities and abilities that make us unique. Therefore, we are also able to deliver extraordinary results, in other words, we all have high potential.

However, there is a lot of unexploited human potential, perhaps because we are dedicating our time to things we don't like or we are not passionate about, thus losing the opportunity to show how truly exceptional we can be.

In the graph below you can see four quadrants combining passion and skills. The idea is that you can find activities for all the four quadrants, not only activities for which you have skills, but also those that you are passionate about. If you find an activity that combines both (top-right quadrant), BINGO!, and if that happens to be your main source of income, SUPER BINGO!

	Try to master it, or adopt it as a hobby	Make your maximum effort to dedicate the maximum amount of time to activities in this quadrant.
Passion		
	Minimize activities in this quadrant	If this is what generates you an income, accept it as such and use it to finance all other things that you are more passionate about.

Skills

The problem is not the lack of enough skills, it is that we do not use the skills that we have. So, ask yourself: What are your talents? What are your passions? Develop your full potential by focusing on that phenomenal strength you have and cultivating it carefully.

Learn from your mistakes

"Information is not knowledge. The only source of knowledge is experience"
Albert Einstein

One day when I was a kid, on a winter afternoon, I was playing with a ball inside my house and accidentally broke a porcelain vase my mom loved. She was not at home in that moment, and I decided to repair it so perhaps I could hideaway the problem. Despite having done my best to put the parts together with glue, it was very difficult to reconstruct the vase and, unable to hide the cracks, it ended up in the trash.

Many years later, as an adult, I learned about a Japanese technique called Kintsugi that consists of fixing the ceramic with a mixture of resin and gold, silver or platinum powder, so that the cracks are covered, but clearly visible. Leaving the scars beautifully exposed, reveals the experiences and battles we went through, increasing their value just by not pretending to hide them. If you google the word "Kintsugi" you will be able to see an image to better understand what I'm describing.

This is a good philosophy that can be applied in life to change the perspective over our past problems, our obstacles, and fragilities, so instead of perceiving them as weaknesses we can see them as a sign of strength and improvement. In this way, our wounds do not disappear, but on the contrary, they become clearly visible and valued when they are covered "in gold".

Kintsugi teaches us to be proud of our scars and to display them with determination.

Adults often lose the ability to accept failure, especially in the work environment where we prefer to be appreciated for never failing, which pushes us to hide our vulnerabilities.

Benjamin Zander, director of the Boston Philharmonic, once said in an interview with USA Today, *"I think it's tremendously important to develop a powerful relationship with failure. If you're a coward and stopped by failure, there's no way to develop. Making mistakes is the most valuable training that exists. My teacher used to say you can't play great music unless your heart has been broken. So maybe the answer is to have more broken hearts and get on with it. That's why I teach my students to celebrate mistakes. Every time they make mistakes I say, 'How fascinating!'"*

People who achieve great things, no matter in what field, understand that failure is not an obstacle, but a milestone on the road to success. Part of the problem is that we get fascinated by other people's success and accomplishments, ignoring the many mistakes and failures they experience on the road to that outcome.

Let's remember some well-known cases to help us visualize this idea of seeing life with a growth mindset:

1. Thomas Edison's teachers told him he was "too stupid to learn anything."
2. Charles Darwin was considered an average student. He gave up a career in medicine and went to school to become a priest.

3. A young Henry Ford ruined his reputation with a couple of failed car business ideas.
4. Stephen King was so frustrated by his attempt to write the novel "Carrie" that he threw away the entire first draft.
5. Walt Disney was fired from the Kansas City Star journal because his editor felt he "lacked imagination and had no good ideas."
6. Steven Spielberg was rejected several times by the School of Film Arts in the University of Southern California.
7. Jack Ma, founder of the Chinese e-commerce giant Alibaba, was rejected from Harvard 10 times and applied to 30 different jobs to which he was also consistently rejected from.

Remember, there is no success without risk and failure. We often don't see it because the result is more visible than the process, so we only see the ultimate success and not the many failures required to get there. Once we understand that success must involve some failure, we stop escaping from risk and challenges.

Strengths

"The real tragedy of life is not that each of us doesn't have enough strengths, it's that we fail to use the ones we have."
Benjamin Franklin.

> *Transcript for a conversation with Markus Buckingham:*
>
> *"We're raised to believe that a strength is what you're good at and a weakness is what you're bad at. If a strength is what you're good at then the person least qualified to identify your strengths is you, because you are not the best judge of your performance. But a strength isn't what you're good at because, let's face it, there are an awful lot of things that you're probably quite good at, that you don't like at all.*
>
> *If you're good at something that's performance, it's not a strength or a weakness.*
>
> *A strength as an activity that strengthens you.*
>
> *A weakness is an activity that weakens you; before you do it you don't want to do it and while you're*

> *doing it, you can't concentrate. That's a weakness even if you're good at it.*
>
> *Strengths and weaknesses are antecedents to performance. If you define a strength this way, as an activity that strengthens you, the person most qualified to identify your strengths is you.*
>
> *If I just told you to take a blank sheet of paper around with you for a week, draw a line down the middle of it and put "loved it" at the top of one column, and "hated it" at the top of the other, and just for a week, any time you find yourself looking forward to doing something, write that in the first column, scribble it down. And then the other way too, in the "hated it" column, write down stuff that you kept on trying to procrastinate, or hand off to someone else, or while you're doing it you couldn't concentrate on. So that you'll end up with a list of "loved it" and "hated it's". That list of "loved it's" is the place to begin when you're trying to answer the question "what are my strengths?". You know better than anyone else does what intrigues you and what engages you."*

Throughout my career I have learned that it's way more important to focus on our strengths than to invest so much time in trying to improve our weaknesses.

Our strengths are a combination of two things, those related to the activities we love to do, and the personality or character strengths. In most cases these two things are related since the thigs we like to do are strongly influenced by who we really are in essence.

One of the key findings about character is that each of us owns a constellation of character strengths that make us different and unique. And even more interesting is that these strengths are universal and valued in any existing culture in the world.

The *"VIA Institute on Character"* developed a three-year project in the early 2000s, involving more than fifty distinguished scientists dedicated to the study of human character. The project resulted in the VIA Classification.

The character or personality strengths are the positive parts of you that influence how you think, feel, and behave, and are a key part of your best version.

According to the study, there are 24 personality characteristics grouped into 6 categories:

Wisdom	- *Creativity* - *Curiosity* - *Judgement* - *Love of learning* - *Perspective*
Courage	- Bravery - Perseverance - Honesty - Zest
Humanity	- Love - Kindness - Social Intelligence
Justice	- Teamwork - Fairness - Leadership
Temperance	- Forgiveness - Humility - Prudence - Self-Regulation

Transcendence	<ul><li>Appreciation of Beauty and Excellence</li><li>Gratitude</li><li>Hope</li><li>Humor</li><li>Spirituality</li></ul>

They are different from your other strengths, such as your unique skills, talents, interests, and resources, because the strengths of your character or personality reflect your "true self", who you really are at your core.

Do you know which of these in the list are your top five? I invite you to take a short test that will help you to rank the character strengths and discover which are the strongest in you. Then you can purposely work to get the most out of them.

https://www.viacharacter.org

Once you go through the test you will receive a report with all your character strengths ranked. Resist the temptation to focus on the bottom of the list, because it's much better that you know what your top five are and strive to show them more often. Even if you don't notice it, your friends and family probably appreciate those top characteristics that set you apart.

According to Dr. Martin Seligman Ph.D., known as the "Father" of Positive Psychology, at work we also must identify our distinctive strengths, choosing a job that allows us to use them daily, or redefining our work so we can use them more.

Deploying our strengths and virtues every day, can not only make our work more enjoyable, but can also transform a routine task, or a dull job into a calling. If those strengths are also our passions, we get the most satisfying and rewarding way of working.

What you can't give up

"In the end, only three things matter: how much you loved, how gently you lived, and how gracefully you let go of things not meant for you"
Buddha

There are things we cannot give up if we want to live a happy life, because they are essential to our personal and spiritual development. Of course, we need money to live, but it makes no sense to left behind everything we love and make us happy in order to earn that money.

If you spend all your time in your work only, and it is not strongly linked to your calling in life, you are neglecting your personal and spiritual growth. Not everyone is lucky enough to work on something they're passionate about, but we must make our maximum effort to get as close to this as we can. If you can't change your job, you should be even more careful with how you spend your free time by making mindful choices.

In one of the "Happiness at Work" sessions I ran an activity with the objective to understand what each participant most wanted to do with their time and with their life. I invited them to reflect about those things they could never give up, those things they couldn't live without. After a few minutes, everyone began to share with the other participants what they had written. The themes circulated mainly around children, spouse, friends, home, music, learning, books, or sports.

Then we spent a few more minutes evaluating how much time we were actually dedicating to those things (we couldn't live without) in our current lives. Unsurprisingly, in most of the cases it was very little, and for others it was simply inexistent. Certain dissatisfaction and even sadness began to emerge in the room. Even a few tears. With certain frustration someone asked: "what we were doing with this finding, and how is this ultimately important if we don't have more time anyway?

The importance, logically, resides in the fact that those were activities or people that belong to our essence as individuals, and they are so important to us that there is no way we can feel complete and be at our best if we don't spend time on them. Without them, we'll most likely feel incomplete, in pain, or simply that we're failing. In fact, ideally, we should make our work compatible with these passional elements. If our work counters or prevents us from doing the things we love, we will end up hating it.

We go through our existence doing a lot of things, trying to fill all our spare time. These days, when our choices are almost limitless, if we don't take the time to think and choose carefully, we could be filling our lives with unnecessary and unrewarding things.

Practicing our passions more often and spending more conscious time with people and activities which we can´t live without is essential in the search of our happiness. There is no happiness without the things that make us happy.

This is not about neglecting our main responsibilities and commitments. Instead, this is about removing from the equation the view of others, cultural archetypes and external approval, and follow our core desires like pretending that we are totally anonymous. From that place where no one sees or judges us, we can think clearly about what we really want to do with our time, inviting us to think about how we make the best out of the time we have.

Whether it's to develop or sustain a relationship with someone we love, starting a new activity, or a personal project, we have a moral obligation with our life to devote time to our passions. To accomplish this, we must also evaluate what we have to stop doing in order to free up time. If we make most of our decisions with that in mind, we will be consciously contributing to our own happiness.

Epilogue: You Choose

You choose. Every day you choose. With every decision, big or small, you choose.

It is through our choices that we create our own reality, because with each decision, we shape and fulfill our life.

You choose what to do with your life.

The best thing we can do as individuals is to honor our core strengths and put them at the service of humanity and progress. To live a full life, we must explore those strengths and passions through which we can transcend and with them, give greater meaning to our life, transforming them into something greater.

Knowing our passions and making choices that bring us closer to them is a way to honor our existence. Whether through science, arts, education, community service, commerce, or any other expression, a full life is about gaining happiness by using our distinctive strengths every day and on as many occasions as possible.

You choose how to conduct through life.

We must take care of our actions because acting impulsively is one of the most common traps we are constantly exposed to.

This idea is wonderfully clear in the following quote, with no hesitation my favorite, a reflection attributed to Viktor Frankl, an Austrian neurologist and psychiatrist, author of the brilliant book "Man's Search for Meaning":

"Between stimulus and response there is space.

In that space is our power to choose our response.

In our response lies our growth and our freedom."

Notes

Notes

Notes

Notes

Notes

Notes

Notes

Notes

www.ingramcontent.com/pod-product-compliance
Lightning Source LLC
Chambersburg PA
CBHW071417210526
45465CB00001B/429